#FrontRowSeat

To Rhonnie

Table of Contents

If you are reading this, I want to thank you from the bottom of my soul. You could have done anything else with your time and money, but you chose to take a glimpse into my life.

Thank you, Heavenly Father, for the gift of writing You have afforded me and the opportunity to share this gift with an audience.

Secondly, I would like to thank God for the parents He blessed me with. Because of them, I am forever grateful for the person I have become and was raised to be.

I hope you can feel a raw sense of emotion through these words, poems, and stories. I hope they paint a vivid picture in your mind as you read. Most of all, I hope you enjoy.

"… so when a man dies all his secrets go with him
and fade, a part of history no longer known.
Done did a lot of dirt, I'll bury with me when I'm gone.
When my story's told, how will they tell it?
Will they say I was a giver, or will they say I was selfish?
Will they say I was a sinner or pretend I was a saint?
Will I go down as a winner, what's the picture they gon paint?
Wouldn't say that I'm a quitter that's one thing I know I ain't.
Will they tarnish, will they taint?
Glorify me, overthink? Say they know me, say I'm great?
Say I'm phony, I was fake?
Say the things about me they never told me to my face?
I was loved I was hated…
I'm a liar I was honest; I was all of these things.
When I'm gone let them talk,
They're discussing who I am.
When they bury me just know I was nothing but a man
wasn't nothing but a man."

– Jermaine Cole

Act One

Act One takes place from my early adolescent years through my high school days – adapting to the everyday life of a teenage boy. Act One shares the internal identity conflict I endured – balancing life in the shadow of a preacher, my father, a spiritual role model, and the challenges of growing up among my inner circle. Along with those battles was the conflict of having to mature faster than most because of trying family circumstances.

<u>Image</u>

"Oh, give thanks unto the Lord..." as my dad greets the church.
You see, it's because of him I've been held to this certain
standard since birth.
I was always viewed as the kid of the preacher who sang in the
choir, jaded by the title like the daughters of Obama had to
acquire.
Sitting in the pews listening to the pastor give his sermon,
reading a text from a girl that says for me she's yearning, while
he talks about how people thought Jesus was scary because he
was a visionary.
This girl behind me in the sanctuary sends a text and says she
likes her style, missionary.
I just laugh and think how this image is so misleadin'.
All these church people wouldn't believe that the preacher's kid
was a heathen.
Thinking about when I was a young me, back in school playing
catch a girl, get a girl, the game we loved to do.
Fast forward to my days in high school. Those went by so fast.
Doing our affiliating handshakes, all day, in between class.
Just young and dumb, living by the motto "Get in where you fit
in."
Then just laugh when the administration thought I was a model
citizen.
Now don't get me wrong, I wasn't terrible by any means, but I
was far from the angel everyone wanted me to be.
So I lived a double life, kind of like Bruce Wayne as the Dark
Knight.
Yea, I grew up with an image to maintain,
and depending on who you ask, the response may change.

This poem is just the intro,
I had to warm you up to me.
I had to use this as the ice breaker so my family and friends
could take me off this pedigree, or better yet, this pedestal
they've always had me.
So, welcome – here's your Front Row Seat.

The Rose

We hear about the rose that grew from concrete, never the weeds
it had to grow through.
Yea, its birth beat death.
And yea, that's a miracle, but how it survived past that is a story
more spiritual.
Long live the rose from the concrete in which it grew because
the story of its survival is only told by a few.

Adolescence

As young boys, trying to prove our manhood was our plight.
We saw it all, from fist fights to when we had a knife pulled on us at the Teen Center one night.
Eleven years old, living like we were grown men.
Lord knows all of the trouble we should've been in, and this will probably be the first time our moms get a glimpse at our life back then.
But I just laugh while writing this because we were some bad ass kids.
But like all things, time ran its course and we grew in our own ways.
Some grew out of the life, and some are still in it to this day.
But from those younger years, you'll always be my brothers; always looked out for each other like Mel Gibson and Danny Glover.

<u>Carefree</u>

Ran this Earth with no cares and no fears.
Scraped my knees up being a daredevil and shed a few tears.
Just a young kid running through the world with more smiles than clowns.
How was I to know by 12 my world would be flipped upside down?
How was I to know that carefree life I lived would take more out of me, at times, than I could give?
Back when I had that carefree life, not a care in the world, truly wasn't ready for the deal that life would serve.

Something to Tell You

I could never forget this day.
I can still hear my dad call out and say,
"KJ, your mom and I have something to tell you."
So, I walked out and headed to your room.
Reflecting on it, I didn't realize or comprehend what was being said.
The only thing I could translate was, "One of your mom's kidneys is dead."
But I was 12 at this time and didn't even know what it meant for a kidney to be dying.
So I asked, "Will she be ok?"
And they said, "Yes."
But little did we know, those years would be filled with crying.
Seeing the pain of my mom struggle each day; if only she knew how much it hurt me more not knowing what to say.
No words to offer that could make it all better.
Just watched as two and half years of dialysis took your spirit away, but you did your best to pull it together.
Maybe you tried to do it for me.
But mama, I had two eyes.
I could see.
Seen all the changes you went through.
Just know your sickness affected me too.
I just think back to that day, and what echoes is what my dad said that day –
"Come in the room. We have something to tell you."

Wonder Woman

What you did, and how you did it, still amazes me.
Standing here on this court, amazed at this site in front me.
How you came to my games, fresh off that dialysis machine,
truly exemplifies how much you're a queen.
Daily, your prince is impressed by how much you press on to
make sure my life is normal like the rest.
While the crowd thinks I'm focused on this shot, I'm worried if
that scholarship is going to come or not.
And with every game, I played roulette with the chances of our
lives staying the same.
Yea, I have hoop dreams, but never visions of the NBA – just
being able to have a college to pay for my tuition, to help
alleviate all the medical expenses.
So I stand here, waiting on this free throw, wishing that the
world could know about my Wonder Woman, my real life super
hero.

Jesus Wept

Just another Sunday, or so we thought.
That call from heaven as we walked in church on March 11,
2007, I never forgot.
You answered, "Hello," as I saw your face change with the
reply.
The hospital had just told you a kidney had become available,
and they had it on standby.
I will never forget the chill that came over my body from that
surreal feeling.
Next thing I knew, right there in the hall of the church, all of my
tears covered me. Nobody could ever know what you had been
through, or how hard it was for me to see you plead to God for
another kidney every night before you went to sleep.
But that Sunday, we shed tears from deep down, from the depths
of our souls.
I feel like when we cried, heaven cried.
Jesus wept for you as we walked out the door.

<u>Second Chance</u>

Hey, mama.
This here will mark 10 years when you stopped having to shed
tears out of the fear that you wouldn't make it through.
You made it to the other side, and as your only child there's no
better feeling than to see the joy you have on the inside of you.
I remember the days I used to wonder if you'd ever see me
married or if I'd place my kids in your arms for you to carry –
The days I used to wonder if you'd make it alive off that dialysis
machine; the nights I cried and prayed that my nightmares
wouldn't become a reality.
You got to see your teenage boy turn into a man, and every day
I'm thankful God gave you your second chance.

Act Two

Act Two fast forwards into my adult years, dealing with my love life from 2015 to the present time, while also addressing societal fragments I have observed.

Act Two comes from the battles of confliction – having the person you love, to that love no longer being there, and you try to move beyond the past in order to move forward with the future.

I found myself, at times, embracing love; other times, hating love because of heartbreak and the internal frustration of living within this current generation.

DM

Hey, how are you?

My name is KJ.

I know you probably get a lot of guys in your inbox, pitching you their best game, their best lines, saying how different they are when really they're not.

Me? Well, I just wanted to introduce myself.

No false promises.

No self-hype.

No "I can do better" talk, no repeated lines, because I'm sure you've heard all that before, right?

I just wanted to stop in and say hi, and I hope you're doing well. And if you give me a chance, I'd love a chance to play show and tell.

And no, that's not some suggestive innuendo to lead to the bed, but me wanting to gain a grasp of the thoughts and emotions in your head.

See, me?

I would love to show you this DM isn't just foreplay to something superficial, but me seeing in you a greater potential – the chance to show you who I am and show you that I care more about who you are rather than how round your ass is or how big your breast is or any of this other generational bullshit.

And after I show you that, there's nothing else to tell you because after my actions you'll think to yourself, "This guy's the truth."

Now here's my number, and hopefully you'll call, and 10 years from now this day you'll recall.

It all started with a DM… because I saw a greater spirit in you than the rest of them.

Retros

What are your favorite J's?
The 1's?
The 12's?
The 9's?
Or how about them 3's?
See, me? I like some comfy 10's.
Some polished 11's.
Some sturdy 13's.
See, this is the same way I feel about our memories.
We had that retro love – that memory for every moment.
For every feeling, there's a shoe for it.
Like when I slide in your DM's, that was that Retro 1 style.
I was unsure of your response.
Didn't know if I'd be rejected, but like a pair of 2's I was gladly accepted.
That Retro 3 feeling was something much more.
That's when you and I could no longer ignore we had become an undeniable force.
You fit me so snug.
So I was like, "I have to have this, of course."
From your laughs to your likes, from your smile to your drive, feeling so good I skipped a couple pair; went straight to that Olympic 7 flair.
That's that gold medal love, girl.
Treated you like Atlas, put you on my back, because you were my world.
My black Aphrodite, my queen, my goddess.
I stood at attention for you while singing praises with my hand on my heart and chest.

That was the high life, but I never felt more alive than when we
had those 9's.

You know… back when everything was black and white.

You were my high-ankle support that kept me strapped tight.

You were the one that broke through my guards like when Bugs
broke into Mike's house in Space Jam that night.

But then, after that 13 feel, we changed.

It was like you got comfortable off the success of our past rings.

Like Valentine's Day 2016 was our 98' 6th game.

Because after that, I retired.

Our game just didn't feel the same.

And even though my infatuation still lasted with your brand, I'm
just waiting for when you made the shoe feel the same again.

Waiting for you to give me that 18 feel.

That you're-back-to-change-the-game feel.

Waiting for you to tell me "This league was mine, and fuck all
them other girls, I'm still wanting to be on the court with you
still."

Now I just think about when we had that retro love.

Now I'm out here alone looking for that retro feel.

Our Last Time

If this should be our last time, our last time together –
The last time we hear each other's voice, the last time to look in
each other's eyes,
I hope from my presence you feel my love. I've always tried to
make you see, and it warms that part of your heart I couldn't
reach.
I hope you hear the radiation of peak affection that comes from
every verb, adjective, and noun I speak.
And when you look in my eyes, I hope you see the spirit of
Cupid that lives in me.
The sincerest emotions that dwell deep. The love for you that
was worn on my sleeve.
If this is our last time together, our last time, just know I still
cherish it like it was our first night.

Thespian

It's crazy how the one person that used to make you smile now
brings a frown.
What's even crazier is that they're the producer of your despair,
but all they can do is smile as if they never cared.
Never cared about the emotions you poured.
Never cared about the sacrifices you couldn't afford.
Never cared about the gestures of love.
Never cared about the extent you went for them... beyond and
above.
It's like a thespian mask, because while one side is happy, the
other side is sad.
The actions bare different reactions, so now we're both just
actin'.
Browning in real life.
"How do I love thee? Let me count the ways."
Well, the ways I showed already, and I'm still feeling this way.
So now I'm left asking about love...
"To be, or not to be: that is the question."
To be indulged and take a chance with love or to sit back, relax,
and just deal with the fact that the love we once had is a thespian
mask.
One side is happy; the other side, sad.

Difference

You ask me what effect you have on me.
To speak honestly, I can't recollect this type of feeling.
So to describe this vibe would be like Columbus trying to explain how the Earth is round.
Don't know how lame that may sound, but just like that man in 1942, there's an ocean that I want to sail to get to you.
Just know the man I am and the energy I give is one I thought I'd never exhibit again.
Well, maybe not again, but definitely for a while because before you I was selfish in my ways.
But everything happens for a reason, right?
The thought I think to myself, laying in these sheets, sharing my inner most thoughts with you at night.
The difference?
Well, you may never see simply because you didn't know the old me.
Just know with you it feels like a verse of "Amazing Grace" because I once was blind but now I see.

Drifting

Cloud Nine.
That's what the term is, but there are so many words to describe
this feeling you give.
Pleasure, joy, happiness, delight.
Yea, there's a few.
But while I can describe this feeling, there are no words to even
match you.
To say you're a queen doesn't do you justice.
These moments of spending days where it's just us, where I'm
seen drifting in your eyes and being lost in your thoughts,
amazed by the spirit and this reality, I never thought I'd capture.
Caught up like I'm Anita, and your love is my rapture.
Drifting, hoping to never stop, and this love never dies of famish.
Until the end of time is the mission that I hope and pray to
accomplish.

Elephant in the Room

An obvious truth left unaddressed.
That's what this is defined as.
So, every day, I open up more of me to you and leave nothing to chance.
On repeat is this Yuna, "Best Love," hoping that the lyrics are you talking to me through song.
Laying here to its soft tune, thinking of you, wondering when you wake up do you think of me, too.
Laying in the bed of your elephant-filled room, but the biggest elephant is you and these thoughts we both share.
Maybe we'll uncover them in a game of truth or dare.
Truth is, well, truth is, I dare myself daily to cherish this opportunity – to dive deeper into this FORTITUDE lifestyle that your life has afforded you.
There's an elephant in the room, and when it finally moves we'll both discover that it's me on the other side waiting for you.

<u>Cherish</u>

I cherish your mind, body, and soul.
I cherish the spirit that resides in you.
I cherish God's hands that molded your shape.
I cherish the angel that delivered you to me and sealed my fate.
I cherish the tone of your voice and the melody that comes from your lips when you speak.
I cherish your smile that goes from ear to ear and that slight crease it forms in your cheek.
I cherish all the small things you think go unnoticed – things like when your eyes change color.
That lets me know what your thought is or how that bottom lip curls down when you put your lips together.
My favorite has to be the way you laugh at my corny jokes or how you fight your sleep at night during our conversations just for an extra minute to stay woke.
See, I appreciate all the little things.
I cherish all the simple things about you, and I just want you to know it's those simple things that truly matter to me.

Dawn

The clock has struck midnight, hours into dusk.
The time when lovers meet and souls touch. The moment when hands speak louder than any words ever could.
The moment our embrace becomes more than what it normally would.
Hearts beating faster than Usain Bolt speed while I pay homage to your temple from your head to your feet.
The moment when fantasies have the opportunities to become reality, and dreams become figments of the past.
How long can the moments last?
How long until the sun covers the moon and its light shines on us in this room?
Well, I don't worry about that.
I focus on this one moment.
I relish in the moonlight that comes through the blinds, and I glance at our shadows, from time to time, that dance all across the wall, praying that the skies never receive the sun's call and there will be no interruption to our dawn.

Forever

Last night, I had you for the moment but what about forever?
What about an eternity of this love we share together?
How about a lifetime of passion sprinkled with the joys?
How about those moments when we're both tired from the toil?
Can this continue like the clouds in the sky, and even through
dark times can we shine like the stars at night?
Can this be forever?
Or is forever too far away?
So I just keep asking, "Can this be forever?"
in hopes you say, "I want this forever."

Perfection

It's hard to fathom if this is real 'cause to never give this side of
me was the deal I made to myself because I gave it all
and lost it all so many times before.
So many L's I've taken, I stopped keeping score.
I learned to not care about anyone but myself.
Block everyone out, be a little more selfish.
But here you are, so perfect for everything I have ever wanted,
but so nervous 'cause I'm worried about this future being
rejected.
Is this to last or will it die?
Will you be mine or will it be a time
that you tell me I'm not the guy?
You've brought out a side of me many have wanted but I could
not express, nor give for that matter, not even cared to share.
But every day I share my mind and visions to you.
Every night I share a connection with you that's so pure and true.
So, yea, I'm nervous because I want my next time to be my last
time.
I want my next love to be the real love.
And from our time together, and this vibe I have with you, I just
hope all of the dreams I have of a lasting connection come true.

No Love in the City

Your smile was the light that took me out of the darkness.
Out of the black alley of the city, somehow you found the
affection no one else could reach.
No love in the heart of the city, that's the old saying, but
somehow the light of your smile reached me and broke through
my denial.
The light now shines bright through the city.
You put love back inside of me.

STeeL City

Just another day in the city where I reside.
Whether it's the Lou or over on the Eastside.
St. Louis, a.k.a STL, but what they're missing are those two E's.
The new age STeeL City.
Not for the production of metals but the reduction of lives deemed fatal.
The STeeL City where your happy night could end up being death on sight.
Not because of any affiliation or hood claim, but because in the STeeL city the hot tempers reign supreme.
The STeeL city that left that baby on the sidewalk while the mom was killed for her Camaro.
Where just walking to your car could end up having you on Fox 2 News.
The STeeL City where we say, "Be safe" every time we leave each other 'cause who knows if the next time I'll see you is with your picture by a news reporter.
Welcome to my city.
Welcome to St. Louis.
Welcome to the East Boogie.
Welcome to STeeL City.

Covergirl

The many faces you hide behind, the insecurities you keep
buried inside.
The hours you spend trying to cover the self-doubt you try to
hide.
You may not do it for a man, but you do it for yourself.
But by doing it for yourself, is it to look good or is it that you
could feel not up to par of the pedigree society has set?
From the wing tips to the foundation and toner, steady trying to
find yourself in this culture like a loaner.
From every commercial to Instagram post, they've made you
question, "Who am I?" and feel not enough without all the
enhancements and being seen with a fresh coat.
Covergirl, uncover yourself.
Wash them shades off and discover your true wealth.
Not wealth in the sense of money and profit, but the value that
resides in your natural.
Let no man, culture, or society define where your beauty lies.
Just know behind all that cover, there's a soul a real man wants
to see inside.

Black Boy

Since birth, even before your first breath on this Earth, your future and character were already foreseen.
It was written what you were destined to be.
A drug dealer, a gangster, either dead or in somebody's penitentiary.
A rapper, an entertainer, a million-dollar baby turned athlete who could only profit from his athletic ability.
From day one, you were made to feel inferior by the shade of your exterior.
You were made to question every job app. "Will they deny me if I check this race box that says I'm black?"
Your style they admire, but it's that same style they label you and make that "just cause" to pull out their gun and open fire, just 'cause.
Black boy, before you come out that womb, just know this world doesn't love you.
They tolerate you long enough to know the power you possess then plot to annihilate you.
But, you just keep pushing, like your mother did that day she birthed you into this world.
But, honestly, black boy, you were safer when your world was inside of her.

Act Three

As men, especially as black men, we are taught to deal with our emotions internally – but never showing anything is wrong. This mentality leads to a high number of mental breakdowns and mental disease within the black male population. Years of unresolved and untouched issues because as black families, frankly, we don't deal with our issues. We sweep them under the rug.

Acts Three and Four will take you on a journey through, by far, the darkest three years of my life starting from the time I graduated college in May 2012. People felt they knew, but no one really understood the emotional toil and anxiety I dealt with during this time. A lot of anger, tears, and depression I experienced and privately dealt with during 2012-2015, but I masked the pain with jokes and laughs. What you will read is the first time I have expanded on this period in my life.

<u>Welcome</u>

I made the best out of every situation.
I hit life with the Tim Hardaway, minus the hesitation.
Made lemonade out of lemons.
Made my own way, never got in where I fit in.
Fought battles within myself, still trying to figure which side is winning.
Had to run away from home, needed to feel something different.
So now I'm here, in the place I always wanted to be, but still searching for that inner peace.
As I wrestle with the memories of the past, I'm always looking to the sky.
"Will I make it to see my future?" type-of-questions I look up to God and ask.
But this life is mine, and I wouldn't dare trade it for the world, except when the world takes away more than I can spare.
But this is my life, and I take the good with the bad, the happy with the sad.
This book is a shovel to bury my past, so put on your black dress and black tie.
I want to welcome you to my life.

<u>Graduation</u>

Caps and gowns.
Pose and smile.
Yea, it's graduation day.
Will y'all please take the picture?
It's 95 degrees out here in the middle of May, but had I known
down the line what was to come, maybe I wouldn't have minded
being in the sun.
But, I'll take it back to '86.
Yea, September 13th, 1986.
That's the year my parents got hitched.
Kim and Kalvin would marry, exchanged their vows, and say "I
do."
Yea, the day my dad told Kim Shari, "I promise my allegiance to
you."
Now let's go back to the present.
July 2012, just two months after graduation, when I found out
your allegiance lost its validation.
To whom it was with, I didn't care.
Where it was at, I didn't know.
All I knew was the allegiance you promised in '86 wasn't at
home.
You cheated the game worse than McGwire, Sosa, Bonds, and
Conseco.
So that day in August, mom and I packed up, we grabbed our
stuff, and we left.
You didn't even fight to keep us there.
You stayed away from the house, and that day I hated you for
that.
You tore our family apart, and you wouldn't let your pride down.

So now it's off to grandmama's house we go, and an unfinished
basement is where I lay my head now.
As I lay in that basement, roll over to sleep with a tear down my
eye, and hear gunshots from over on 22nd, thinking no longer is
my 10x10 the room I sleep in.
If only I could go back to graduation.

Exiled

The day she became an Outkast.
Not glorious like Big Boi and Andre 3000.
More like when Simba banned Kovu from Pride Rock to the
Outlands.
It was amazing how the feelings toward her switched.
You went from calling her sis to acting like she didn't exist when
she had been around you long before that 13th day of September
1986.
It was you she told about his acts so egregious.
And you who told her, "Girl, you need to leave and get away
from this."
But when she left, she couldn't believe the ones who called her
sis would start to ignore that she even exists.
Because of someone else's infidelities, she's the one that got
slandered and exiled.
Then there's her son who, as an only child, observes how his
mom has been cast away
and left isolated like Tom Hanks on that isle.
He sees her breakdown with tears at night and sits in a hospital
room as her health declines.
Because what she thought was family, exiled and slandered her
in the blink of an eye.

Borrowed Time

"Partially functional.
Half of me is comfortable.
The other half is close to the cliff like Mrs. Huxtable" as my
stereo plays that "Friday Night Lights", J. Cole, "Too Deep for
the Intro."
As I ride in this rain, riding down Interstate 64, doing 73, I look
out my windshield, and in my rearview I see Luci in the
backseat.
She asked me, "What's the deal. You just goin' to sit there and
cry? Why live in pain when you could just die?"
I tell her shut up as she replies, "Nah, now you're on my time.
Years ago you should've been died.
You're on borrowed time.
Remember on 70, on your way to McKendree, when your car
swerved on a rainy night like this, and you missed that semi,
head on, by just an inch?
You should've been dead in a ditch, but God blocked me then.
But now I got you to myself in this dark rain again.
This is the sequel, and this time I will get this win.
You're up here crying 'cause your daddy doesn't call you.
Boo hoo.
You can shed those tears as wide as the Mississippi.
Fact remains, I been waiting for this for years, and this time it
won't miss me.
Your daddy doesn't want you and your mom's sick.
Don't you see, you're the common denominator in all of this.
If you were never born, your mom wouldn't need a kidney
transplant.
Your dad would've been left.

Don't you see? You're just dead weight.
Just go ahead swerve this into the median for all their sakes."
"No!" I said. "Go!"
"Didn't you hear me the first time?
You on borrowed time.
In 2012, you should've been mine.
There's nothing working for you on this side.
You can't even keep it together.
Look at you, doin' all that crying.
You're on borrowed time.
And I'm here to collect.
So stop stalling, 'cause tonight you will die in a wreck."
I fade out Luci, and I hear that final verse of "Enchanted."
I turn the music up and the lyrics I start chanting.
Music for the soul that saved mine that night.
I looked back at Luci.
Not tonight.
Guess you lost this battle.
God beats Luci another time.

Sleep Talking

"Hey."
Yea, I hear you, but what am I going respond for?
You haven't called since we moved in August.
Why you bother to come around for?
"KJ?"
Yea, I hear you, but I'm going to lay here in this bed.
I heard you coming in from upstairs so I cut off my lights and put the covers over my head.
I have nothing to say to you, you coward. You let us leave and destroyed our family like World Trade Center towers.
"KJ."
What?!
Don't you see I'm not talking?
Just 'cause you're here to see us on Thanksgiving, you expect me to be happy or something?
Nah, I'm going to lay under these covers and ignore your presence and give you as much time as you gave your efforts.
So you can keep calling my name, or go back upstairs, or just stand there and stare at the TV, I don't care.
"Aye, Kim. He's sleep."
Trust, she knows better.
I was just with her, but what can she tell me?
To heal the pain that you cause me to suffer?
You chose another life over me and my mother.
And for that, my anger won't die.
I just deal with it and never let you see me cry.
No use in crying over spilled milk or showing love to a man who just let his family dip without no call to check up on me to see if I was drowning in misery.

Nah, you chose your side piece over your own family.
All these thoughts going through my head on the day I'm
supposed to give thanks.
The only thing I gave thanks for during Thanksgiving was that I
didn't take my life instead.
Sleep talking like a zombie in this bed.
Dying on the inside, angry on the out.
Sleep talking, lips quivering from every emotion I want to shout.

Reconcile

Pulling up to your driveway, not sure of what I'm going to say.
Thoughts still unsure 'cause nothing could prepare me for this
day.
Feeling like Cory in "Fences" because over time my only
defense has been my pride and to keep all this anger built up
inside. But mama told me God can't bless me if I can't forgive
you and look you in the eyes.
So I walk in, sit down, and tell you all of my hurt.
Laid out all of my pain you caused trying not to spill a tear on
my shirt.
When I was done, you just sat there with your legs crossed as if I
was the one to blame for my despair.
But even though you never said you're sorry, I had to realize the
words you spoke would be the closest I would get probably.
In our own ways, I guess we both felt the toil of our schism, and
we just dealt with the discomfort with our own coping
mechanisms.
And that's pride.
Your pride was hurt, and mine was torn, too.
So now here we are, trying to piece our relationship back
together like arts and crafts in school.
Will it ever be perfect?
Maybe not, but this father-and-son love is something neither one
of us could stop.
So I just wanted to say, "I love you" knowing that you love me,
too.
Missing those calls when I'd pick up and you would say,
"What's up, dude?"
Because no matter that the affairs are true,

I want this to be the day we turn the page and have a part two.
So now the story continues.
Miles Davis trumpet couldn't play a sadder blues.
"Little Boy Blue" still playing his calmest tune.
Show me you love me.
After all, you named me after you.

Phoenix

You were my escape.
Those nights with you were my moments to get away.
Your pain replaced the pain of a shattered me.
Your toil replaced that of which I felt from my family.
You were my Goliath I faced like David,
and you forced me to be strong like Samson with loads to lift.
Embedded, embedded, embedded.
That's what you became in me.
Until one night, it became the realization of a dream.
For this reason, no one can ever understand my pride for our
relationship because I had you at a time in my life when I felt
like I didn't have shit.
To you I'm forever grateful – grateful that you are forever a part
of me.
When I felt alone, you became my family.

Close Call

No winter could've gotten colder than that January, or was it
February?
Honestly, I don't remember 'cause I was too concerned with
your health if you'd live to see November.
I saw you in that hospital bed, and although you were well, I
couldn't help but think that I probably could've lost you...
damn.
Looking out the window of that room, thinking of all the time we
wasted and wondering if your demise was coming soon.
So I had to let you know another time how much you meant to
me, and without you I don't know where I would be.
And for the first time in my life, you opened up to me.
And I wish there was a camera there that could've captured the
expression on my face.
Crazy how it took a close call for us to finally get to this place.
But everyday I'm happy for that moment, 'cause who's to know
the unturned stones
we would've left if not for us exposing our emotions to one
another.
The tears I shed as you said sorry for the trouble you caused my
mother.
The phrase "I love you" you had finally spoken.
As I got up, you mirrored my actions, extended for a handshake
and then a hug after.
And as I left you there that night, my heart sank in my stomach.
My throat too tight to swallow, trying to hold my tears back
while walking down that hospital hall, but when I finally got to
my car like a baby I bawled.
It took 24 years for us to have a moment like that.

Took almost two years to get our relationship back.
Took a moment for both of us to be scared, that you would be
heading to those Golden Gates, for us to finally have that
exchange.
I cried because I wish it had been Sooner like we lived in
Oklahoma.
But everything happens for a reason, and I'm just glad I was able
to have that moment.

Act Four

Act Three puts you in the middle of a horrible situation, but like they always say, "time heals all." Maybe my dad and I needed that time. Originally, Act Three and Act Four were one act, but there's a great deal of emotion in Act Three, and a break needed to be had because Act Four only puts more on your plate.

Act Three ended in February 2015.

Act Four fast forwards you to May 16, 2015, and I take you on a 13-day journey I will never forget.

Time Table

I'll never forget that day Erika called,
"KJ, your dad's in the ER."
My world stopped, I quickly left work, punched the gas, and sped off in my car.
Once I arrived, I saw you were the same.
You seemed fine, but within 15 minutes I picked up on the change.
Because I'm your son, I caught it in an instant while everybody in the room looked at me with a puzzled face.
I reiterated, his speech has changed.
I told the doctor, "My dad doesn't speak like this here. He was speaking just fine 15 minutes ago, and now there's a lisp after every word I hear."
I could see it in your eyes.
You looked at me like, "How did you catch this?"
And once you spoke again, the nurse could see my reaction.
As my mom sat across from me, I reached down to grab my phone and I texted her, "I think daddy had a stroke."
Then it was confirmed by the doctors the same day, and now a stroke victim was your label.
Not knowing today would be the first of your six-day timetable.
May 16, 2015, I was part of a life I'd never have believed I would ever live.
Day after day, I came to the hospital and saw less and less life you had to give.
I saw you go from talking and laughing to having to vacuum the saliva out your mouth to keep you from gagging.
It was all good just a week ago, but a week you didn't even make it.

And I sat by your bed, daily, to see pieces of you fading.
May 21, 2015, your body gave up the fight.
Those six days will still plague my mind for life.

<u>Demise</u>

Never did we think Superman would ever die.
And no matter how many tears Lois shed, he still came back to
life.
I'll never forget the day the doctor said that you wouldn't
survive.
Out of 24 years, that was the first time I ever saw tears come
down your eyes.
That was more powerful than anything I could have ever seen.
For the first time, I saw Superman in a state to where he was
weak.
At that point, the stroke crippled you from speaking, so the only
way to express yourself was the tears that trickled down your
cheek.

Demise Part 2

Mom said, "KJ, your daddy is reaching for you."
So, I grab your hand and you squeezed it tight and I felt a slight pull.
That's when I looked into your eyes.
You looked back into mine, and we both could see inside our time together was soon to be over.
Soon the tears fell as if they were leaves in an autumn October.
And we cried to together, similar to the O Jays, but there's no Eddy or Gerald Levert. Just the pain of us knowing your time was coming and you'd no longer be on this Earth.
The next day, you laid there, not moving, not talking, but the machines said you were still alive.
Even though you showed no life, your spirit was still living inside.
So I had to make a choice that was really tough.
In front of all the family, I had to say I've seen my dad go through enough.
Rather than see him suffer, I had to tell them to pull the plug.
The day after, God took you to the heavens above.

Bed Thoughts

As I sat there on the bed, in the room, in the house you, mom,
and I once called home, I couldn't help but to think of all the
things that went wrong.
Couldn't help but wonder did you suffer the night you had a
stroke?
How Auntie Lawanda and Uncle Kevin found you in the house.
Were you unconscious?
Were you woke?
I sat there in that bed realizing I just watched my dad pass to
heaven hours ago.
Now I'm just trying to hold it together and let no emotions show.

Phone Call

Shon pulls me to the side.
"Hey, your mom had a bad day.
While we were cleaning the house, the other woman kept calling
and harassing your mom with words to say."
What was ironic is I noticed my mom had been acting different.
My dad just died, now she's being harassed by his mistress.
She has a lot to deal with.
So, I tell my mom I have some errands to run when in my mind
I'm headed to the house to handle this.
I drive up and walk in the house still eerie from my dad not
being there and it being empty.
I walk to the phone and scroll through the caller ID.
I see this frequent caller, and I said let me call her.
She says, "Hello?"
I say, "Hey, this is Kalvin."
She begins to talk to me as if I'm him, but I cut her off, and say,
"Nah, this Kalvin Jr. As in his son."
I began to exchange some words with her I'd rather not repeat
but I said, "You've been harassing my mother for years, and now
this time you're speaking to me."
She begins to deny all the accusations as if I'm dumb or if I
don't have the evidence to see.
Then her whole tone changed when I told her don't call here
anymore, my father is deceased!
Click, I hung up the phone, sat in that house and cried alone.
If those walls could talk they would repeat the echoes of those
tears as they hit the floor.
Felt like I was crying for my dad, but I was crying for my mom
and my own soul.

The one thing my mom, dad, and I buried, I had to face head on.
As I cry, the phone continues to ring, and it's her number that
keeps showing on the screen.
I wipe my face and look around for my keys.
As the phone continues to ring, I realize I did what I had to do.
It's time for me to leave.

Bold

Before my mom and dad had their moment, I remember my
mom saying years ago, "Side chicks are the boldest."
I laughed, 'cause to hear my mom use the word "side chick" was
amusing.
Years later, I'd have to find out for myself the truth in that
amusement.
Facebook comes across my phone and says you've got a
message.
Some more spam is what I'm initially guessin'.
Nah, it's the mistress again.
Not only did she send a message but also a friend request
notification.
Yea, my mom was right.
These side chicks are pretty bold because in this message she
begins to unfold things to me that were never told.
So I call her from my cell to get her off my case, but she starts
off by saying, "Please, let me explain."
Now this is where shit gets deep.
My dad just died three days ago, and now she drops all this on
my plate to eat.
Like how her and my dad met in college, and she got pregnant,
how she loved him, and how it hurt when she had a miscarriage.
And I'm listening on the phone with my mouth to the ground,
and I'm dazed in a stare.
Because at this time, him and my mom were a pair.
I remember my mom saying how she used to regularly visit him
there.
I reflected on the story of how my dad left to come to school
back home to be with his mom.

But maybe it was his other life he was running away from.
And reading this you could think, "It's just the other woman
trying to get up under your skin."
But I read the texts in my dad's phone that night to confirm it.
All I could think of is all the trips my dad took for work to
Dallas in the 90's.
Just so happened to be where she lived, ironically.
Outraged from it all, I yelled into the phone, "You were a side
piece then, and a side piece you have always been.
He didn't marry you, he didn't love you. Only used you like a
car and gave you back when he was through.
By the way, weren't you married, too?
Yes, ma'am. I did my research on you.
So this will be my last time I say this.
My dad is dead, so whatever business you had, it's through."
Click.

Barely Above Water

Trying times.
That's an understatement to define the times from the past week.
From dealing with a mistress and now trying to find a dime to
bury your dad in time.
Financially responsible wasn't my dad's strong point, and no life
insurance policy made to help lessen the burden.
So now I'm left here to rub together coins. Trying to make a
dollar out of 15 cents, but it's just not cutting it.
Stressing to my mom, what do I do?
There's no money to give him a funeral.
Do I ask the church?
Do I ask my frat?
But my pride wouldn't let me even choose to do that.
So I had to swallow my pride and ask my family to help.
Sitting there in front of them asking was the most helpless
moment I ever felt.
Feeling like a bum on the corner begging for a quarter to get a
soda out the store.
Sitting there glancing around the room. Looking at us, looking at
each other, while I'm choked up trying to get out that there's no
money to bury my father, their brother.
As if that isn't bad enough, my phone is still buzzing.
My family sees the distress on my face and
someone speaks up to say, "KJ, I'll put in on something."
Then another.
And then another.
Still feel like my head is barely above water.
Now the weight of that is lifted, but like the old saying, "If it's
not one thing, it's another."

Final Call

Two days until I bury my dad, and one hell of a week I've already had.
However nothing, and I mean nothing, could compare to this call.
The other woman calls me again.
"What?" is how I answer the phone.
Instantly, I'm shocked by her calm tone.
Then she proceeds to say, "I just want you to know I'll be at your dad's funeral."
Now you can only imagine the words I said, but in summation I told her it's better for her to stay in Texas instead.
She goes on about how she wants to pay her respects and see my dad one last time.
Mama said these side chicks were bold, but bold isn't even a word to describe this move.
So I asked her, "You come here in front of my mom and me, and you think that's cool?
I tell you what. Fly out here if you want to, clown, because I promise you, you'll be carried off and cuffed before your feet hit the ground. How's that sound?"
Click.

Funeral Day

Woke up stressed beyond belief.
So much on my mind that morning I don't even bother to eat.
Worried about if this woman is going to show up and cause a
scene at the altar.
More importantly, worried about the protection of my mother.
I meet my family down at my aunt's to wait on our limos.
As my cousin pulls up, I ask him, "Are we all set to go?"
Right on cue, police cars pull up on the block.
You would've thought my dad was a slain cop.
But me, I made arrangements with my cousin and my prophyte
who are both police.
I told them the day before I need extra security.
My mom, not knowing anything of the woman, the phone calls,
or even the threats, just thought it was my cousin's gesture on
putting his uncle to rest.
Butterflies as we pull off from the house. You would've thought
I was Obama.
After every block, heading to the church, was a cop car on the
lookout like we're a caravan protecting him from the Taliban.
We pull up.
I step out.
Scanning the outside of the church checking to see if she's here.
I help my mom out the car, grip her hand, and pull her closer.
I walk in church as we wait in the hallway and make sure
everything was okay before we arrived.
Shake some hands, give some hugs, and before I know it, it's
that time.
Time to see my dad for the first time since he passed.
Time to say my final goodbyes before they close the lid on the

casket.

The weirdest funeral I'd ever been to. Because rather than focus on the fact I was burying my dad, I'm looking over my shoulder trying to see where in this sea of people is this woman at.

Is she here?

Did she come?

Or did she stay home back in Dallas?

This, mentally, has been a challenge.

Now it's my turn to give my eulogy of my dad.

Through that rough year we had, and all that happened this week, nothing could ever replace what he had been to me.

I speak words from the deepest corner of my heart.

Choked up on some memories because never at 24 did I think I'd bury a parent.

Or at least I thought.

But even with those words.

Standing in that pulpit, looking at family and friends that had supported us through this, I couldn't help but focus on those words that were said two days ago.

"I'll see you at your dad's funeral."

So as I speak words, my mind and eyes are in another place.

Scanning the crowd, wondering if she's shown her face.

Watching my mom and making sure there are no conniving glances at her.

As we left the church, I could finally take a breath, but the cemetery put me at an even more unrest.

So many people came out.

It was hard for me to know who was friend or foe.

As we sat there at that casket, I felt so exposed.

Couldn't tell who was behind me, but more importantly, who was behind the woman who gave birth to me.

So, as a son, my Spidey senses start tingling. Couldn't focus on, "Ashes to ashes and dust to dust."

I was too busy looking to see who was on the left, right, and in back of us.

Soon, the dust settled and it was all the past.

We got back in the limos and headed back to the repass.

You know, what black people call the meal after the funeral to help ease the pain you feel after you've just buried your loved one six feet under grass.

Now I can close this chapter because everything went okay, but to myself I'm thinking, "If people only knew what I went through this whole day."

Will and Testament

"If I should die today."
After writing this, there's still a message I must relay.
No lawyers.
No legal counsel.
No attorneys.
Just a few last words after I've already given you the last of me.
"If I should die, I pray my brothers know what they've meant to
this single child."
How their bond helped me through my roughest times and kept
me with a smile.
"No homo" or "pause" is ever needed to be said.
Just know your little brother loves you all, and in the case of my
death keep the memory of me in your head.
If I should die young like the good are prophesized to do, I pray
my Godson never forgets my presence.
And while I chased ambitions out in California and Dallas, I
always prayed for you and that your mom could get it together so
your life could be normal at last.
If I should die young, like G-baby in hardball.
To my family, I don't apologize for telling it all.
I had a story to tell to answer God's call.
I hope that you understand.
But even if you don't, the only thing I hope is that I gave
someone else going through similar situations a little glimpse of
a chance.
If I should take my last breath, and death snuck up on me in
stealth.
To my cousins, I'm forever grateful for the bond we share.
When I went through my hard time, you were the only family

who reached out or even gave a care.

Because of you I stayed around, but I just couldn't fake it anymore.

If I should die before you'll ever get to dig into my soul, just know, mama, I left this world ready to go.

I'm thankful for all of the strength you showed.

From you being sick from your kidney disease to dealing with dad's infidelities.

And to you being forced out of the family.

Thank you for all you did and sorry for all I didn't.

Thank you for the love and belief.

And I'm sorry for my selfishness and my grief.

If the good Lord takes me today,

I pray I'm able to reach that place where I can, again, look my dad in the face.

Smile and give him the hug we shared before his spirit left the hospital that day.

I imagine hearing him say, "What's up, man?" when he sees me at the gate.

I would thank him for allowing me this story I was able to serve to you, to get these emotions off of my plate.

To God, I'm sorry for all those times I wanted to play God and shorten my life in all of those dark times and seal my own fate.

I'm thankful, someway, somehow, your voice reached me before Luci.

This is my last will and testament at this point.

I leave no riches behind, but if I die, I die a wealthy man with the bonds and love I keep inside.

I pray my memory brings a smile to someone's face.

I hope my presence, my voice, and my actions cross your mind, day to day.

I just hope I'm never forgotten, and hopefully from this piece I can remain in your hearts and minds until the day you're deceased.

Lastly, I pray that this book leaves the imprint of a young man who felt trapped but dug deep down and tapped into a higher power that freed his mind, body, and soul.

I wrote this for you to know someone goes through your battles, too.

Never feel you're alone.

THE END

Dedicated to my father: Kalvin Jeffrey Hilliard, Sr.
December 12, 1959 – May 21, 2015
Until we see each other again.

CPSIA information can be obtained
at www.ICGtesting.com
Printed in the USA
LVOW10s1019161017
552601LV00015B/310/P